AF580326

ERIC FISCHL
Sculpture

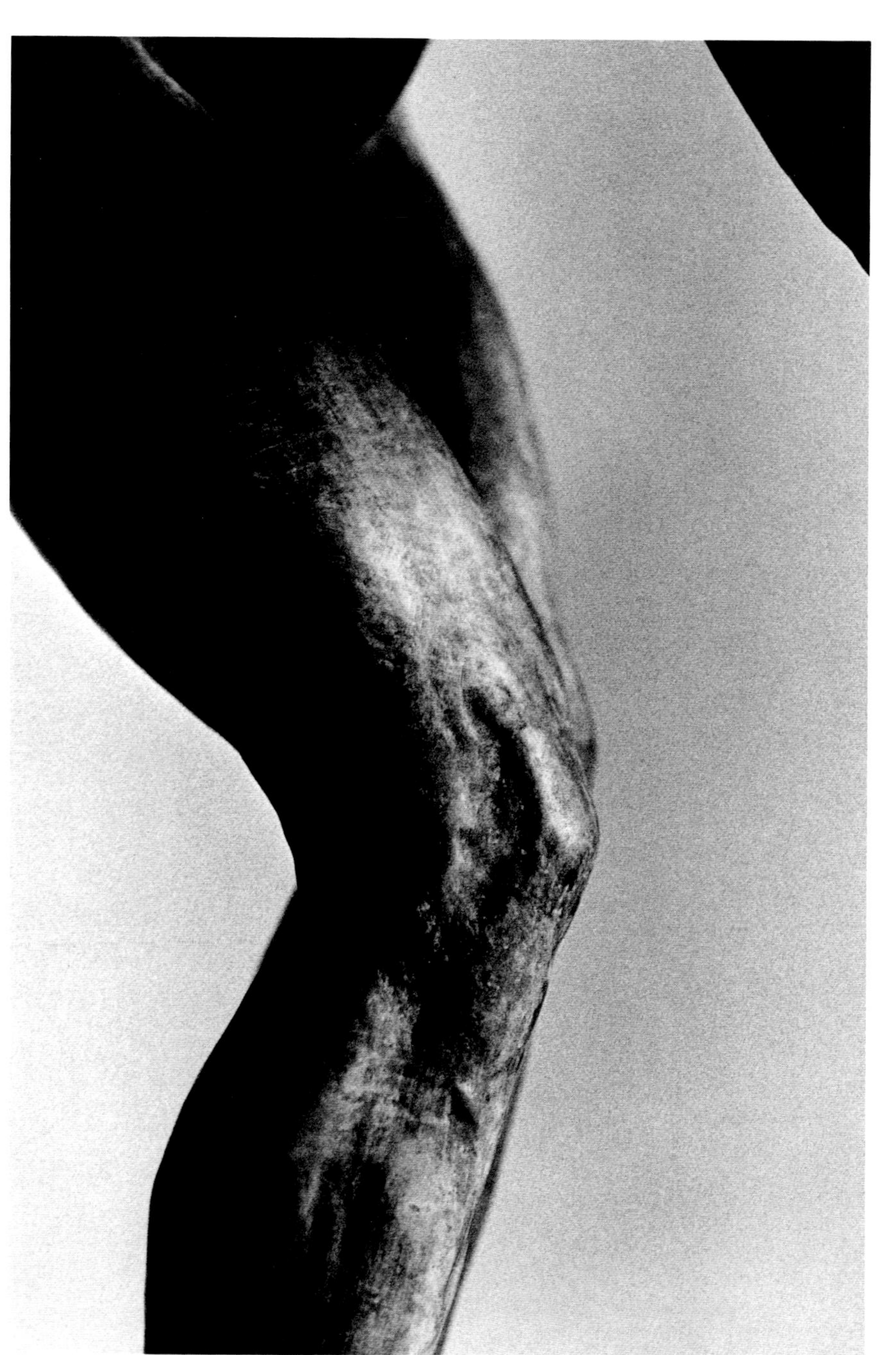

ERIC FISCHL
Sculpture

A CONVERSATION ABOUT SCULPTURE WITH
ERIC FISCHL AND EALAN WINGATE

PHOTOGRAPHS OF THE SCULPTURES BY
RALPH GIBSON

GAGOSIAN GALLERY
NEW YORK
1998

A CONVERSATION ABOUT SCULPTURE

WITH ERIC FISCHL AND EALAN WINGATE

How did you come to sculpture?

ERIC FISCHL: I started innocently enough. I had been making paintings derived from photographs I took in Southern France, and I was needing to reenergize my painting. I found that there were certain characters that would keep reappearing in the paintings and drawings. They became almost like a theater group.

EALAN WINGATE: *A repertory company.*

I became so familiar with these people from this one position in my photographs — I knew them from the back, for example — that I wondered if I could imagine them in three dimensions. What would their fronts look like? I wondered how well I knew them. I got some clay and began to make these small sculptures. Once I had made one, I'd put it on a table in the studio and then I'd make another one; over the course of weeks I had made several. One day I looked over at this table, and it looked like one of my beach scene paintings. All the characters were there.

So one way that you turned to sculpture was in the assistance of painting.

Yes. It was actually to reinvigorate my paintings which had become all too familiar to me. I wanted to be more expressive with the way I drew and painted. I thought if I copied the sculptures I had made I would achieve that effect. You see, the sculptures were relatively crude and disproportionate. The distortion was built in already. Also they were made with gray clay so I would have to invent color and that might free up the way I had come to see color.

And did that work?

At that time I made several small paintings derived from the photos I had taken of the sculptures. It was an odd, convoluted process: photo to sculpture to photo to painting.

The real results came a few years later when I made a series of paintings that benefited from what I had learned from the small works — paintings like *Brother and Sister, Nick's Picnic,* and *What There Is Between You and Me* — where I distorted the scale to create a more charged psychological scenario. It also started me making more sculpture.

What have you discovered is the difference between sculpture and painting?

A painting can have the slightest reason for being initiated. It can have a simple reason for existing. But sculpture, no matter how small, is about monumentality. Painting may stop time but it doesn't always monumentalize it. Painting also controls its context. It has its own light and space and scale. It disappears when you no longer look at it. Sculpture, on the other hand, must compete with everything that surrounds it. It has its own internal scale but it is greatly affected by what else is around it.

That's about looking at sculpture. What about the making of sculpture or painting?

The making of sculpture is fundamentally different from painting. In painting, it is the hand that follows the eye. In sculpture, it is the eye that follows the hand.

Is that being said from a point of view of someone who's been painting for so many more years than they've been sculpting?

No, I think it's that sculpture is so much more about the hand in the making, the feel of it, and the stored information that's in the hand, in relationship to the body. That is, the hand having touched so much so often knows things that consciously you didn't know you knew about: the anatomy, the feel, the weight of something, the gestural stuff. And so your hand actually leads the way, and then your eye compares it to what it knows. With painting it's sort of like your hand is moving to catch up to what your eye is seeing, because the eye is looking at something here, and putting it here.

It's not about touching, it's about having seen and seeing again.

When you were capturing people with photography and later putting them into paintings, you always seemed fascinated by their body language and your fantasies about them at that moment. Do you find the sculptures are as effectively capturing this body language pose or are the figures in a moment of transition?

First let me say that I make a distinction between pose and posture. A body posed is really about abstraction. It is about formalism and not about emotions or psychology. Posture is quite different. The posture one's body assumes carries with it all the memories of its experiences. These memories bend, twist, stiffen, and overemphasize. Posture, like sculpture itself, is indelible. It is this sense that the way one carries oneself is the result of an epic struggle between internal forces reacting to external forces that I find so compelling in the works of artists like Michelangelo, Rodin, and Giacometti. It is a quality I strive for in my work.

I'm interested in the sculptures in which you seem to torque the air around the figures, which maybe at the one point gives them their sense of stasis or repose, and, as well, their moving gesture. So there is this jumping back and forth between the two notions.

I love that idea.

But these people, or statues, are wrapped up in their own activities. They're noncommunicative.

I don't understand. To me they are very communicative. At the very least they communicate discomfort.

The female figures seem to be internalizing their grief. They are imploding with what they're dealing with, while the male figures are externalizing with greater ease.

It's ironic because usually the stereotypes are the stoic man and the hysterical woman.

But both ways of expressing, regardless of gender, are universal — just reversed from the classic stereotypes we expect. I'm trying to get to the gripping sense of modernity these sculptures express at this moment at the end of the twentieth century. Is it discomfort they convey or isolation?

Think about these sculptures as if you were witnessing people in a state of torment over some irrevocable consequence. Their isolation is part of that consequence. Their physicality reflects it.

My work has always been concerned with those moments just before or just after something occurs. I try to give the viewer the feeling that what they are witnessing has significance and is not arbitrary or coincidental. I am not a formalist. I am aware of the issues of formalism, but I am not interested in emphasizing them. I don't care how flat or how massive or how geometric the volumes are in space. What fascinates and inspires me is that we can make likenesses of ourselves that are so animated it is we who become frozen in our awe. It is we who become sculpture.

I can't help but think there is something quite primeval, even biblical going on in this work. As we are becoming the sculpture, are we as well participating in a morality drama about "the fall" from grace?

Allow me to make a statement which I find compelling. There are three categories for content in art: heaven, hell, and the garden. These three archetypes occupy different places within the creative imagination. Artists at one time had to be able to be expressive and inventive in all three, but in this century, what with specialization, artists are usually conversant in only one. Though these categories are derived from the Judeo-Christian mythology, I do not mean to imply that artists today are making religious art. What I do mean is that these categories are metaphors for ways of understanding various forces within life and within art. They hold in them our ideas about order and chaos and desire. They are about harmony and union and dissonance and isolation and perfection and resolution, etc.

I have always been a garden artist. I prefer the garden because it is not fixed and immutable. It is life in a state of becoming. It is a place where an individual can still make a decision.

To get back to your question, what is compelling about "the fall" is its inevitability. It is about choice and about separation. It is about the loss of innocence. It is about the moment in which you see life as uncertain, filled with hardship and conflict and your choice is irrevocable.

Is that also the inspiration for Hysterics of Love*?*

Hysterics of Love was inspired by something I read in passing. The author mentioned that Mary Magdalene had put ointment all over the dead body of Christ and then wiped it off with her hair. I realized that I had never seen an image of that event portrayed, though there are many portraits of Magdalene with a jar of ointment.

So it is a gesture of total supplication and of total selflessness.

It is complicated. Yes it is about supplication and selflessness, but it is also an image of hysteria. It is the language of profound grief bordering on madness. It also seems terribly erotic. I tried to create a sculpture that was sufficiently ambiguous so as to contain those contradictory elements. I think the viewer will first see an image of eroticism and love-making and then also be reminded of Michelangelo's *Pieta.*

Being reminded of Michelangelo, how do you deal with the influence exerted by previous sculpture over your audience?

I am always struck by the certainty of art criticism disapproving of Rodin as a precedent for contemporary sculpture.

What do you take this to mean?

I take it to mean that the world has changed so much between then and now that he is of no value and cannot be considered a source of inspiration for artists working today. I wonder what has happened since then. Something so profound must have occurred that fleshy, powerful, sexy, emotionally-expressive bodies cannot be used to contain meaning today. Don't forget, after Rodin the next sculptor of note was Giacometti, who basically finished off the figure with anorexia — self-loathing so fierce the body is eaten away from the inside out. After Giacometti it has been body-casting all the way, which is a technique that comes from the death mask. I think we are a death-obsessed culture. Not death as another state of existence but rather death as absence and loss. Think of the art object as a corpse. Artists have gathered around the corpse, stunned by its inanimate physicality. We discuss its deadness and come to represent it in like terms. We impress ourselves with our observations about its flatness and its sheer weight! We are amazed by how unresponsive it can be and demonstrate this by poking it, hurling it around, amputating parts. We cannot get over its lack of luminescence and so brighten it up with colorful lights. Nothing we do to it changes this one immutable fact: It is dead.

Is that the way you feel about art?

I have never been able to buy into thinking that the tradition of painting and sculpting I inherited was essentially damaged or possibly irrelevant. I have always felt sure about the expressive viability of these mediums. I have always believed in their communicative powers. I have always trusted in my hands.

When you see or think about previous figurative sculpture, do you feel a similar kinship with the hand and the eye of those sculptors as with your own?

Yes. But I must say it is the hand that has suffered the

greatest abuse in the art of the twentieth century. It has been the object of such scorn, anxiety, and disappointment. It is, after all, the one thing in art which betrays our presence. And it is the presence of the human touch that has become so problematic. This has actually compelled me to try to make more sculpture — to see if there was a way of accepting Rodin and using Rodin and doing something that wasn't Rodin.

What is Rodin to you?

I love Rodin. You can go right up to his sculpture and it becomes this other level of appreciation because it's so handfelt, handmade — you reenact the making of it with him as you witness the sculpture itself. Even though the gestures are often corny, the corniness is overcome by the power of his sculpting. The expression that he brings to the surface and the scale that he deals with is so overwhelmingly right: it's abstracted and symbolic.

What Rodin had was an absolute belief in the body — and the body was its own context. It was a sacred form, so that anything you did to it became meaning. If you made it into an exquisitely beautiful and sensuous surface, it could hold that, that belief in that.

And so the body was to Rodin what the canvas was to the Abstract Expressionists in the fifties. If you did not believe the canvas was a really true representation of the world, then you were not going to believe that anything they did in terms of smashing, scraping, ripping, would have any meaning at all. And that's what Rodin was doing with the flesh when the body was still something to believe in. He was the last great sculptor of fully-fleshed, fully-expressive human form. He brought us a confrontation with our physicality unlike any since Michelangelo.

Our discussions have remained in Europe somewhere between Rodin and Michelangelo. What effects do you see from your extended stays in France and, more recently, Rome?

European cities are populated with sculpture. Statuary is everywhere, and everywhere you turn you see the human form represented. It makes you feel at home. It is populated by the memories and glorification of those that have gone before and set the standards and shown us how to behave. It is us honoring ourselves.

In Rome, where so much sculpture is placed on columns and domes and roofs, you can see in that beautiful light of their gorgeous sunsets these warriors, heroes, seers, and saviors come to life like celestial beings flitting across the sky. It is such unabashed fantasy, such spectacle, that you cannot help but be charmed and amused and inspired by it. I love all these representations. I miss statuary. I wish there were more people making it and more places to put it.

ATELIER

PHOTOGRAPHS BY RALPH GIBSON

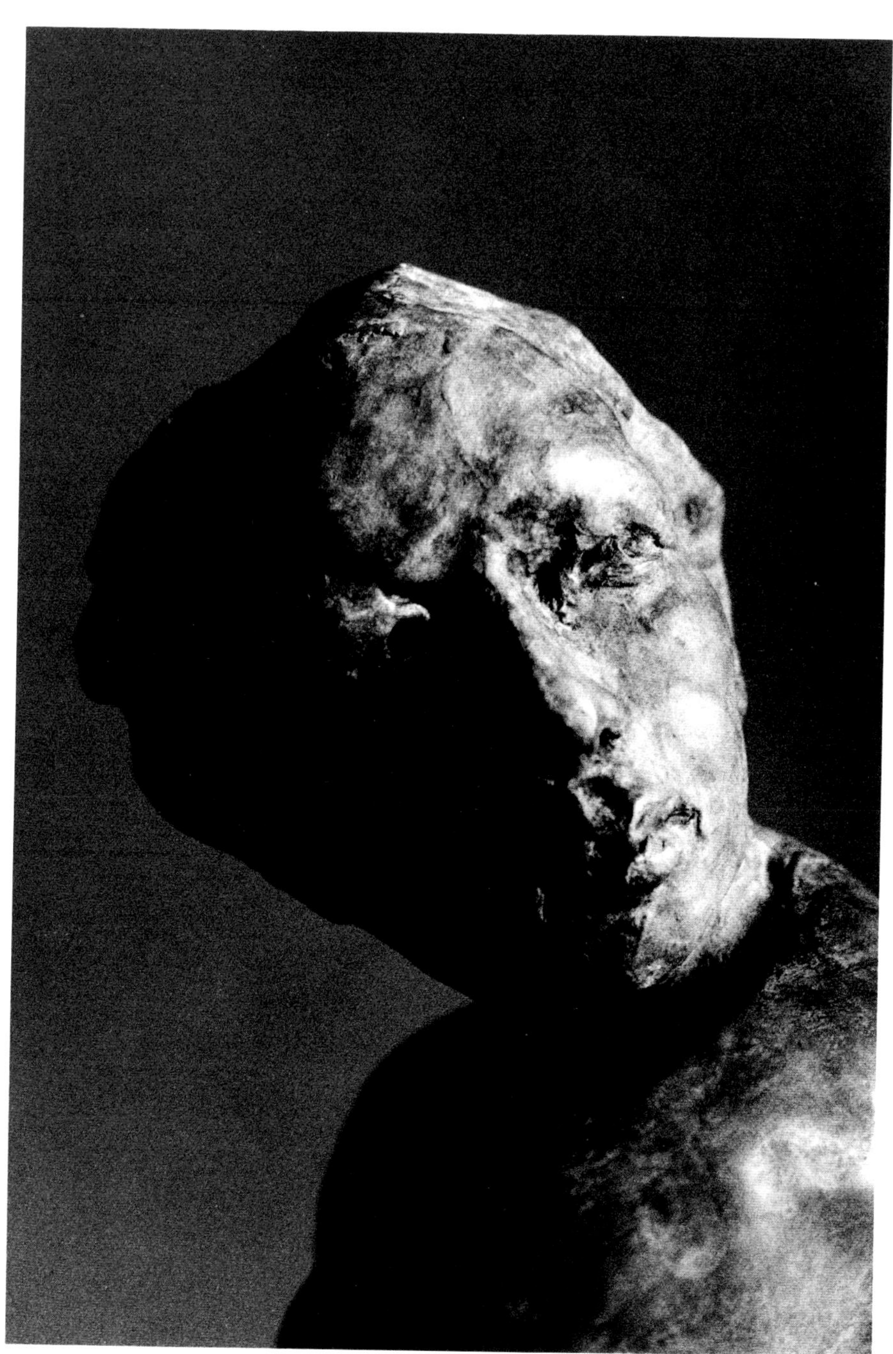

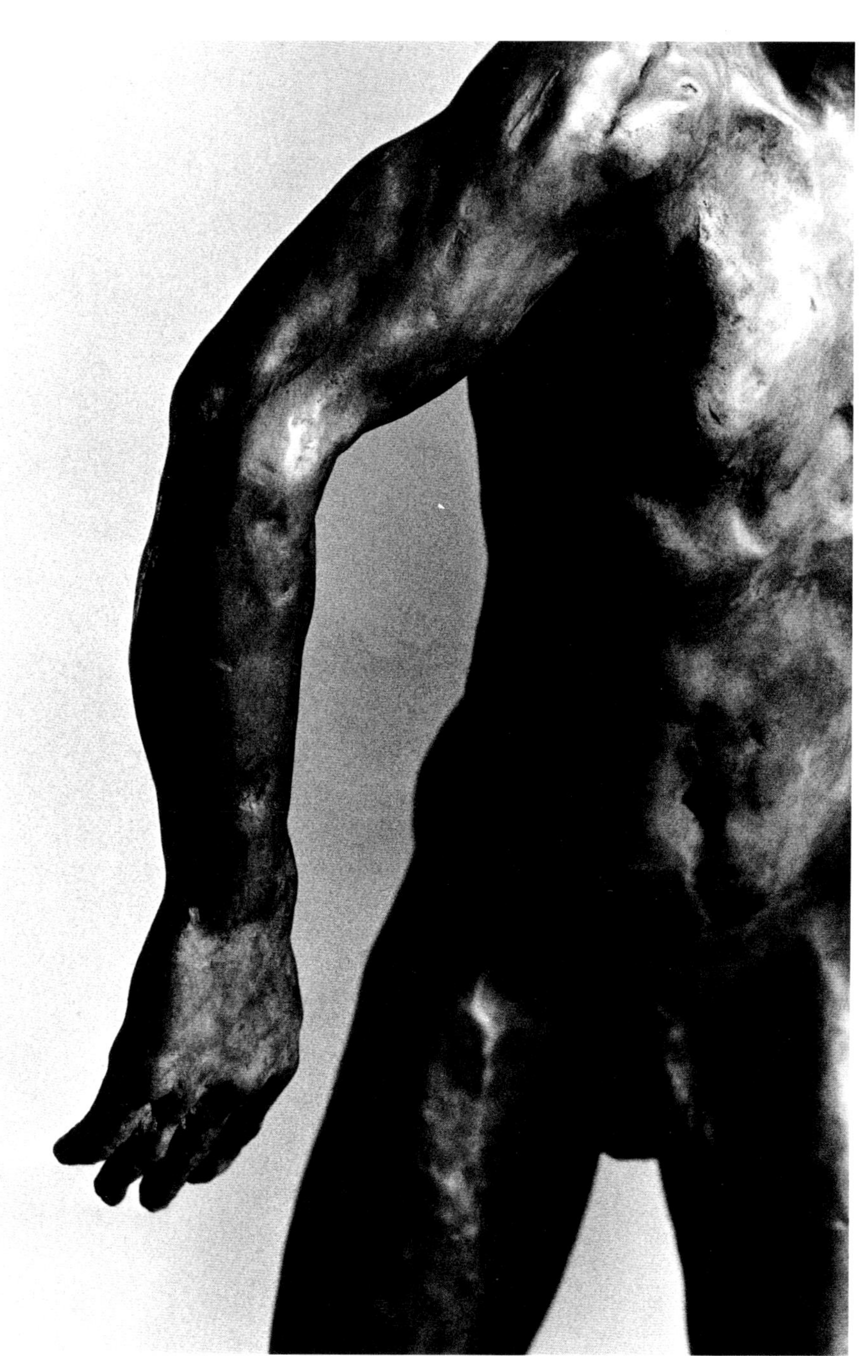

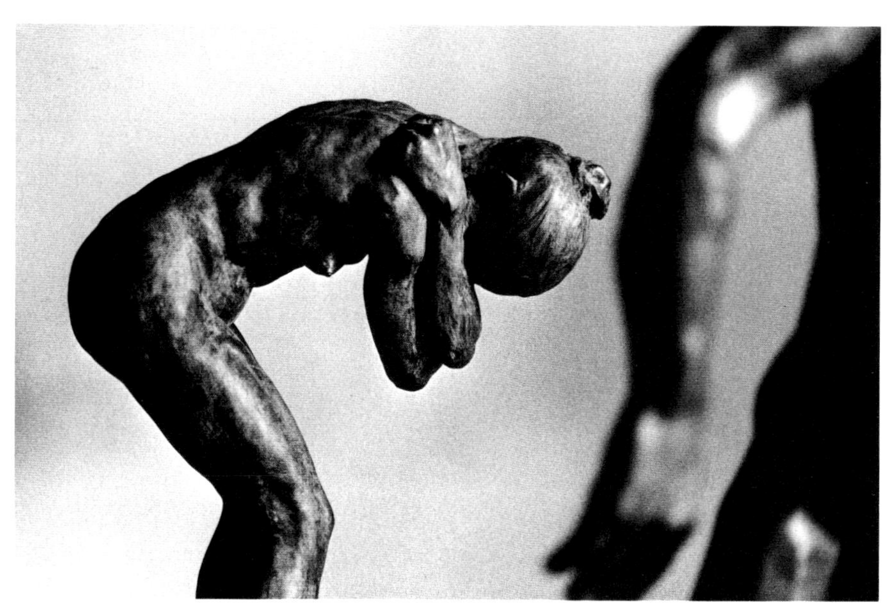

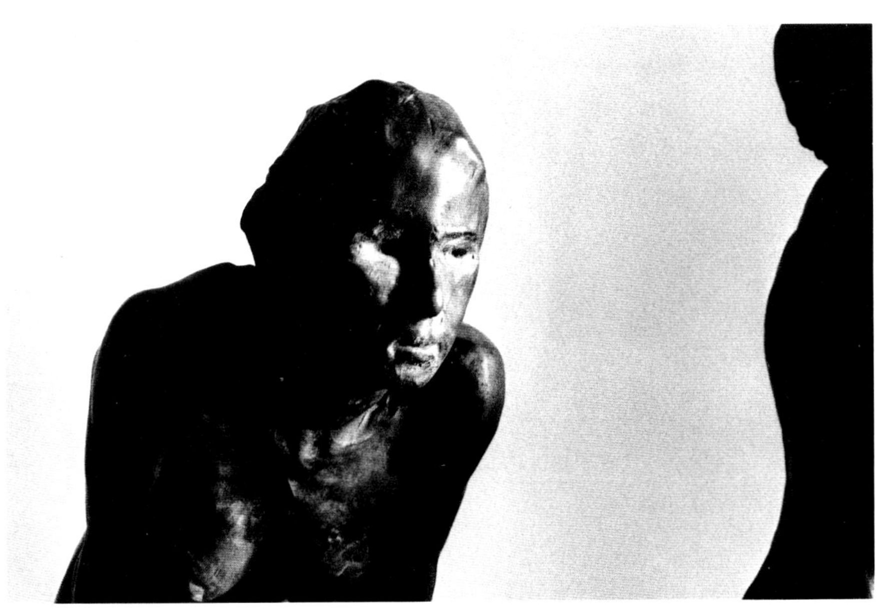

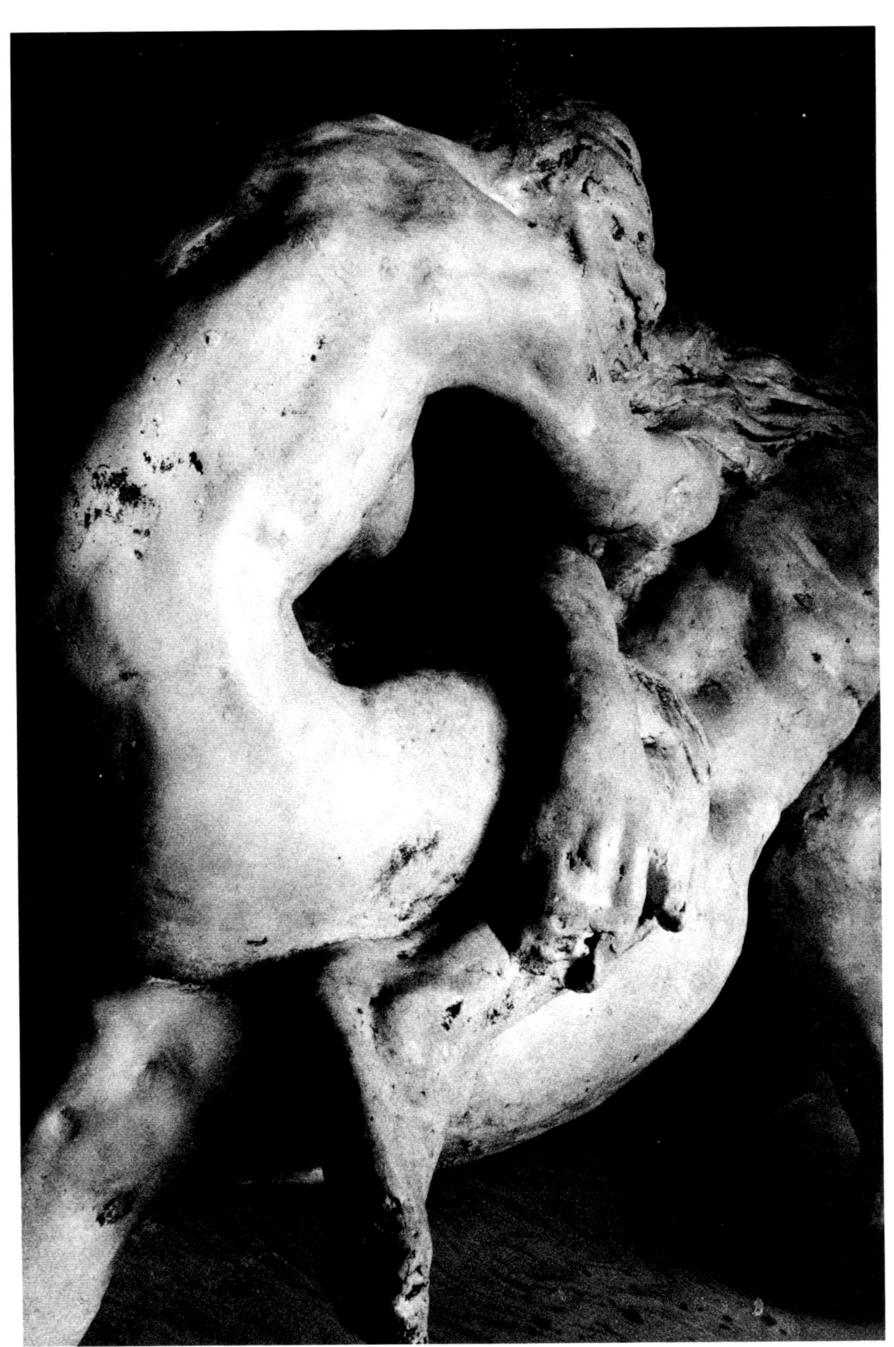

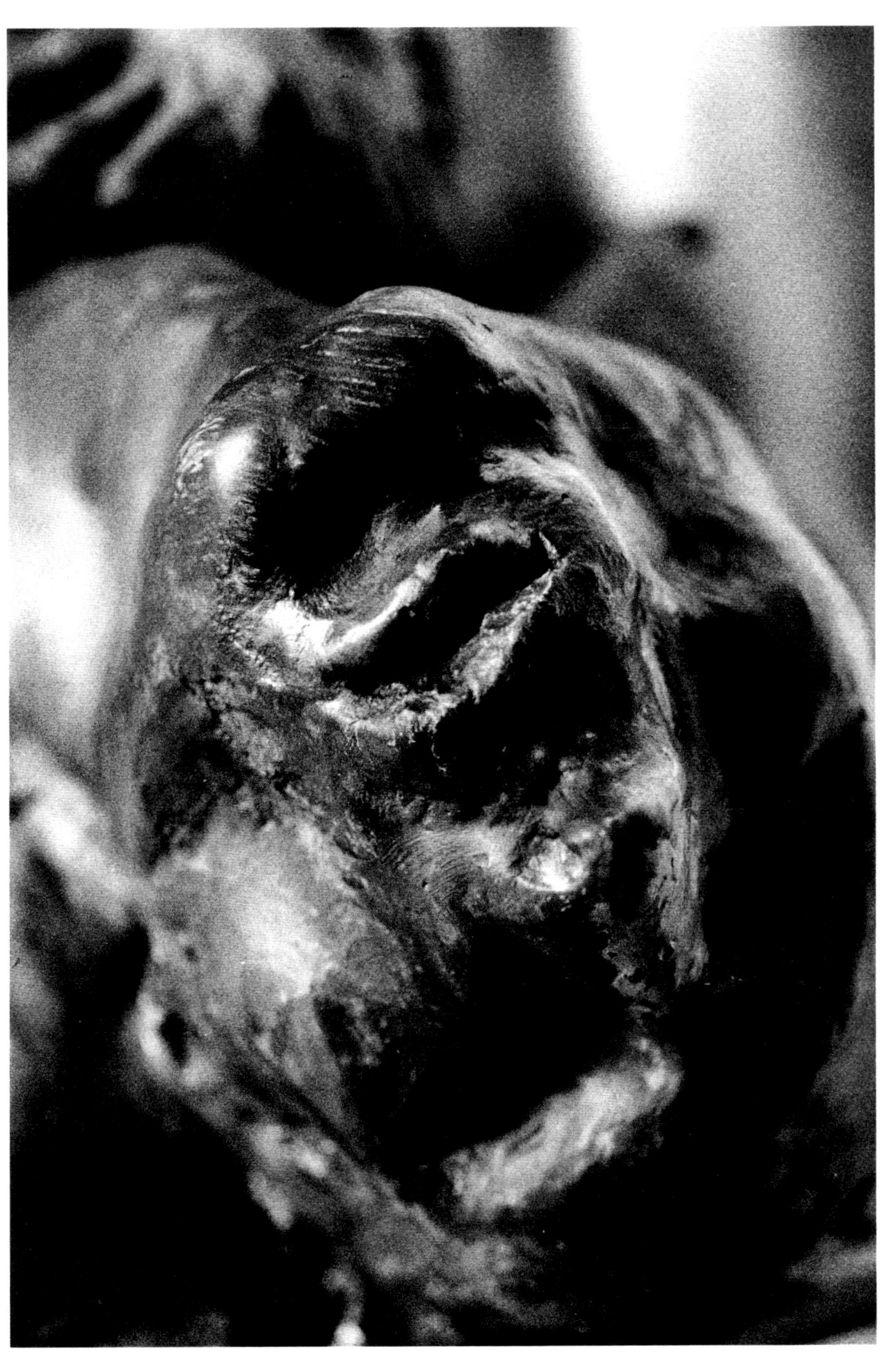

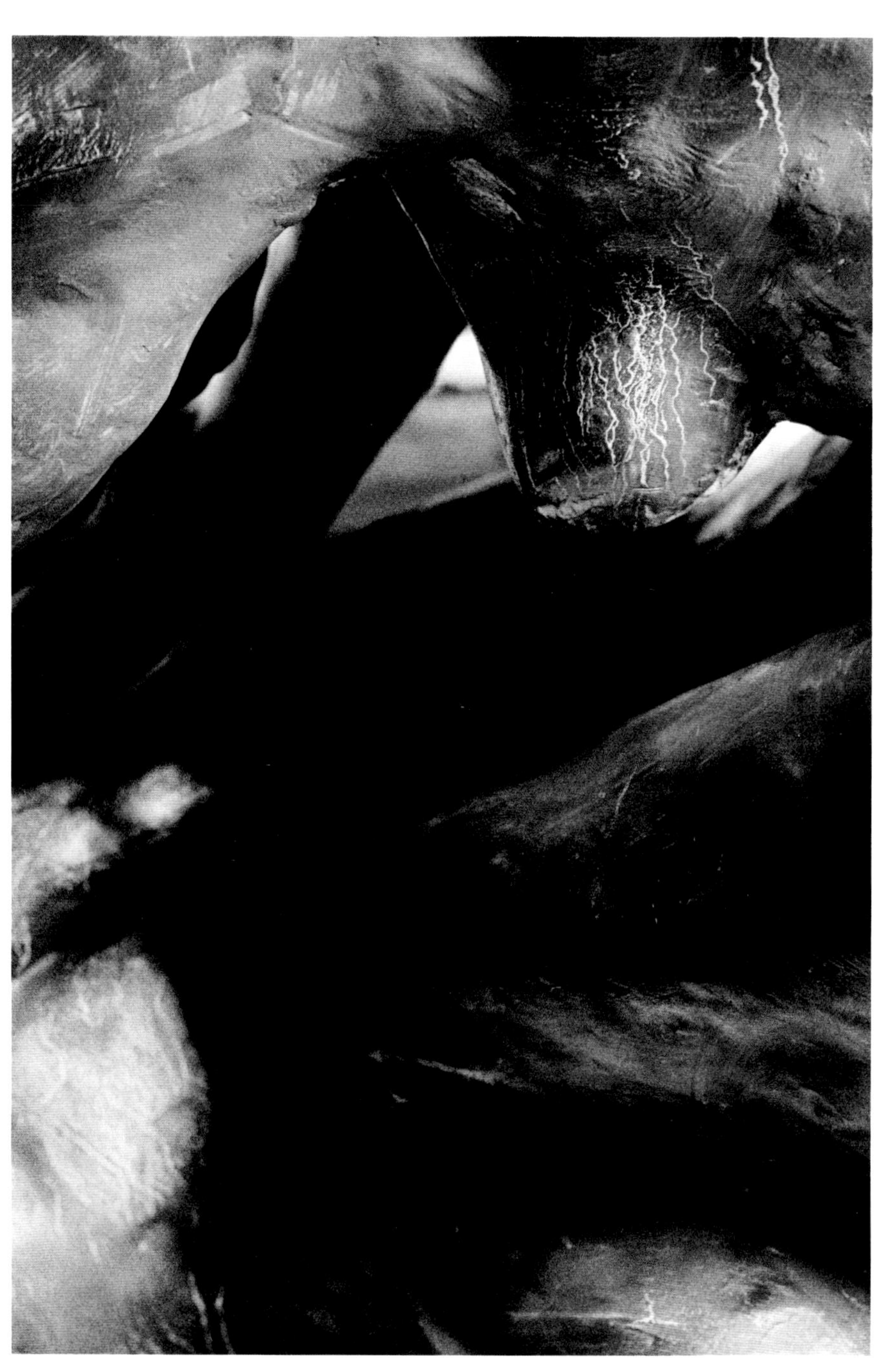

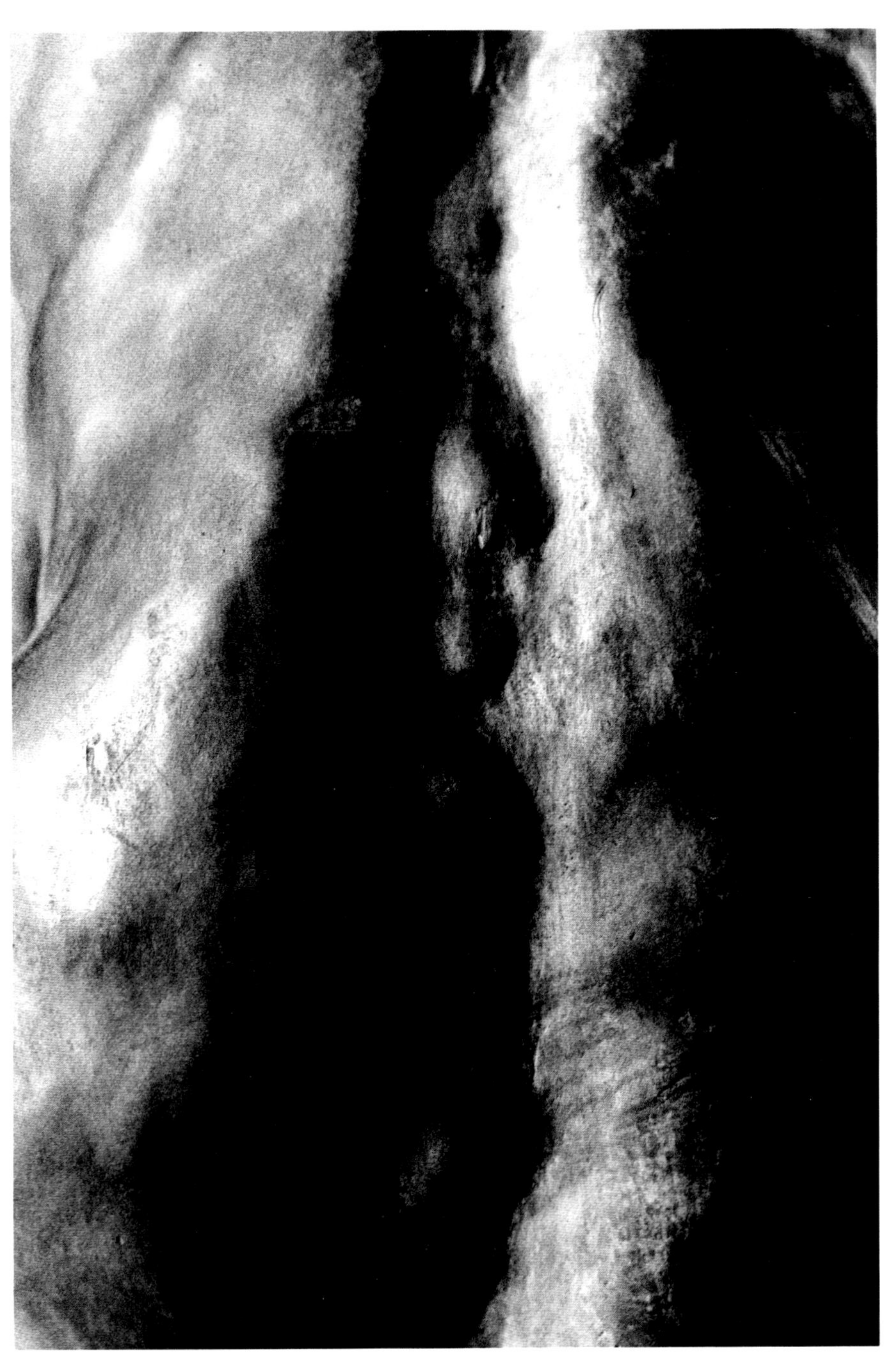

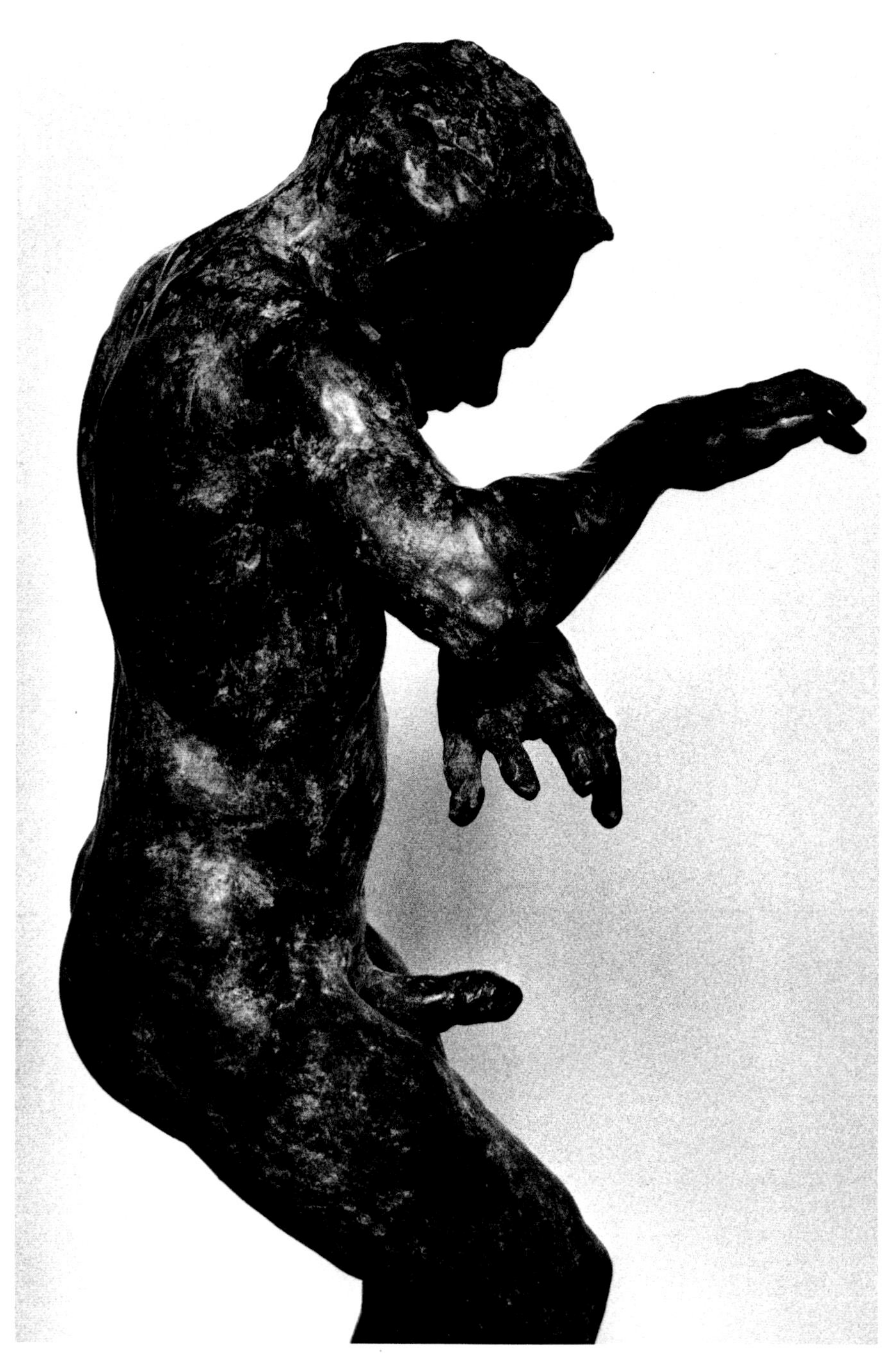

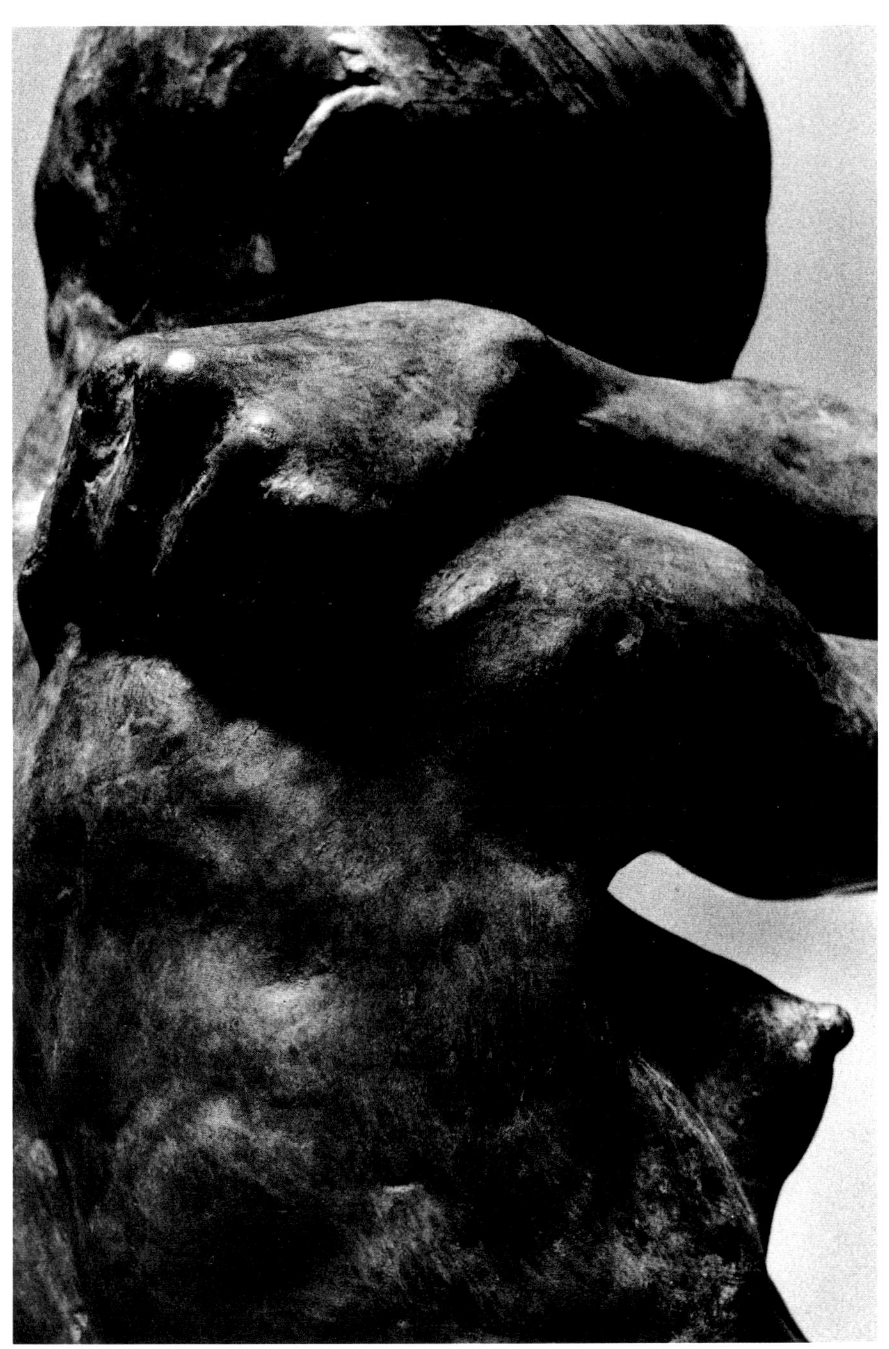

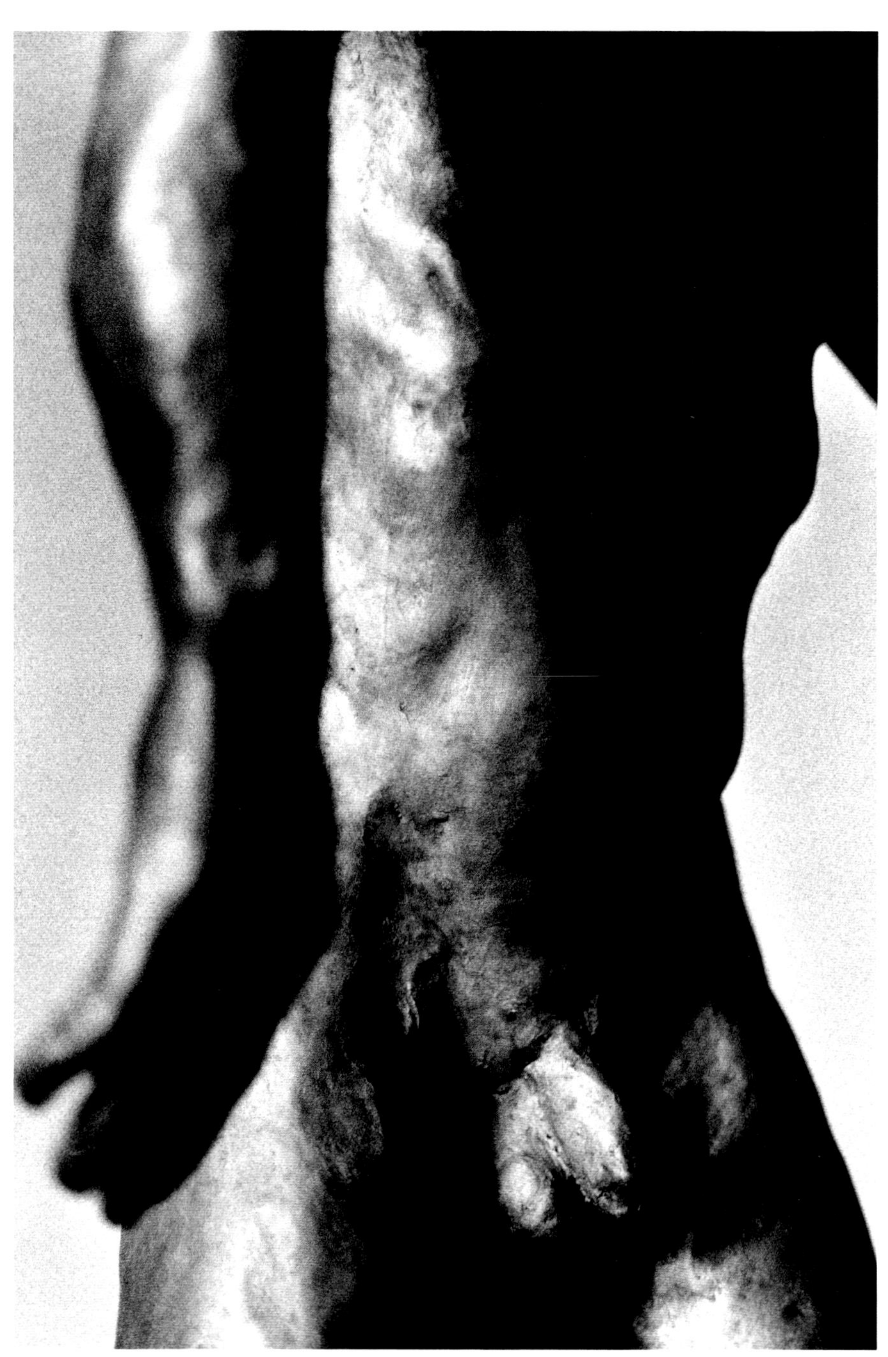

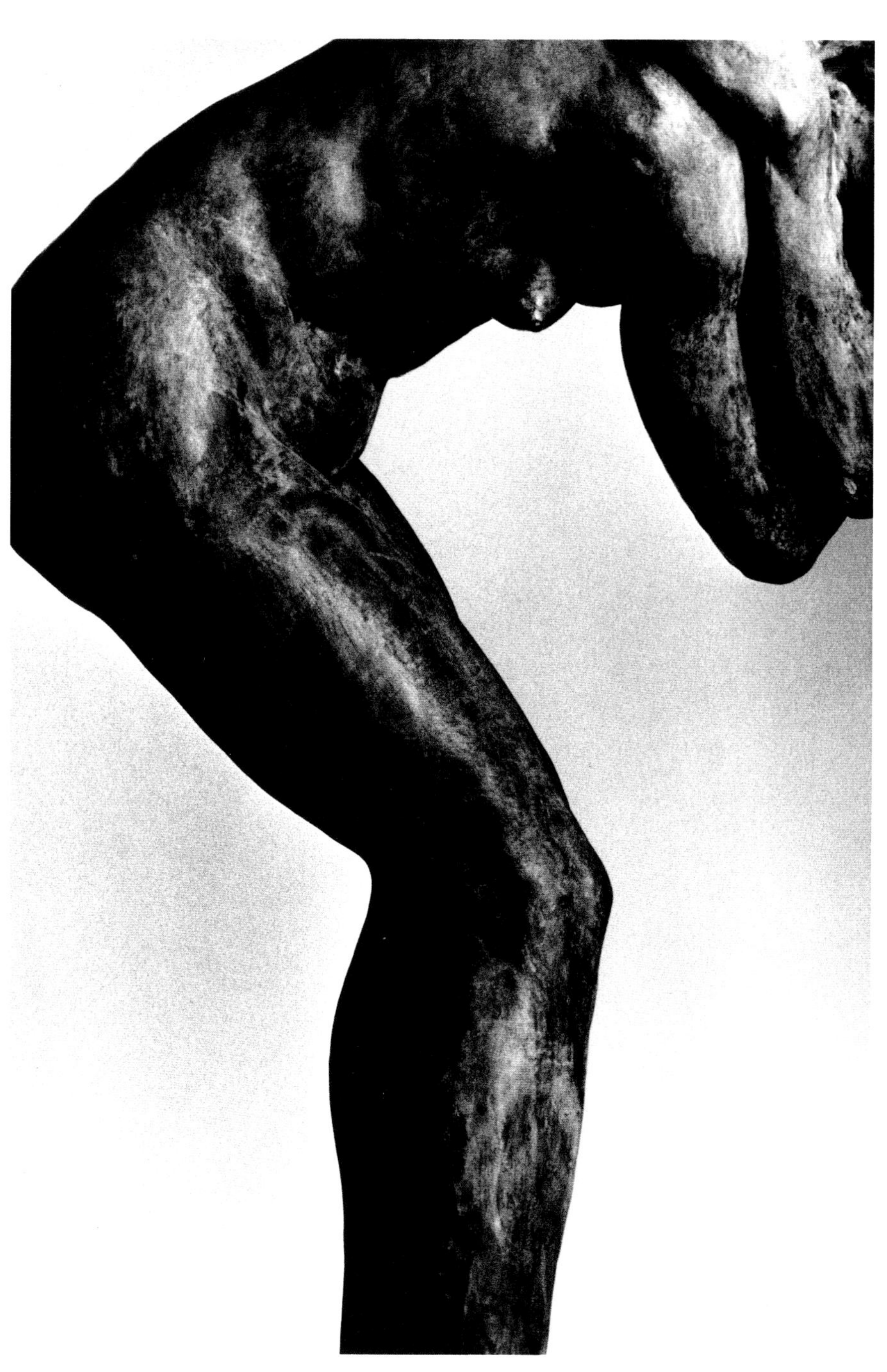

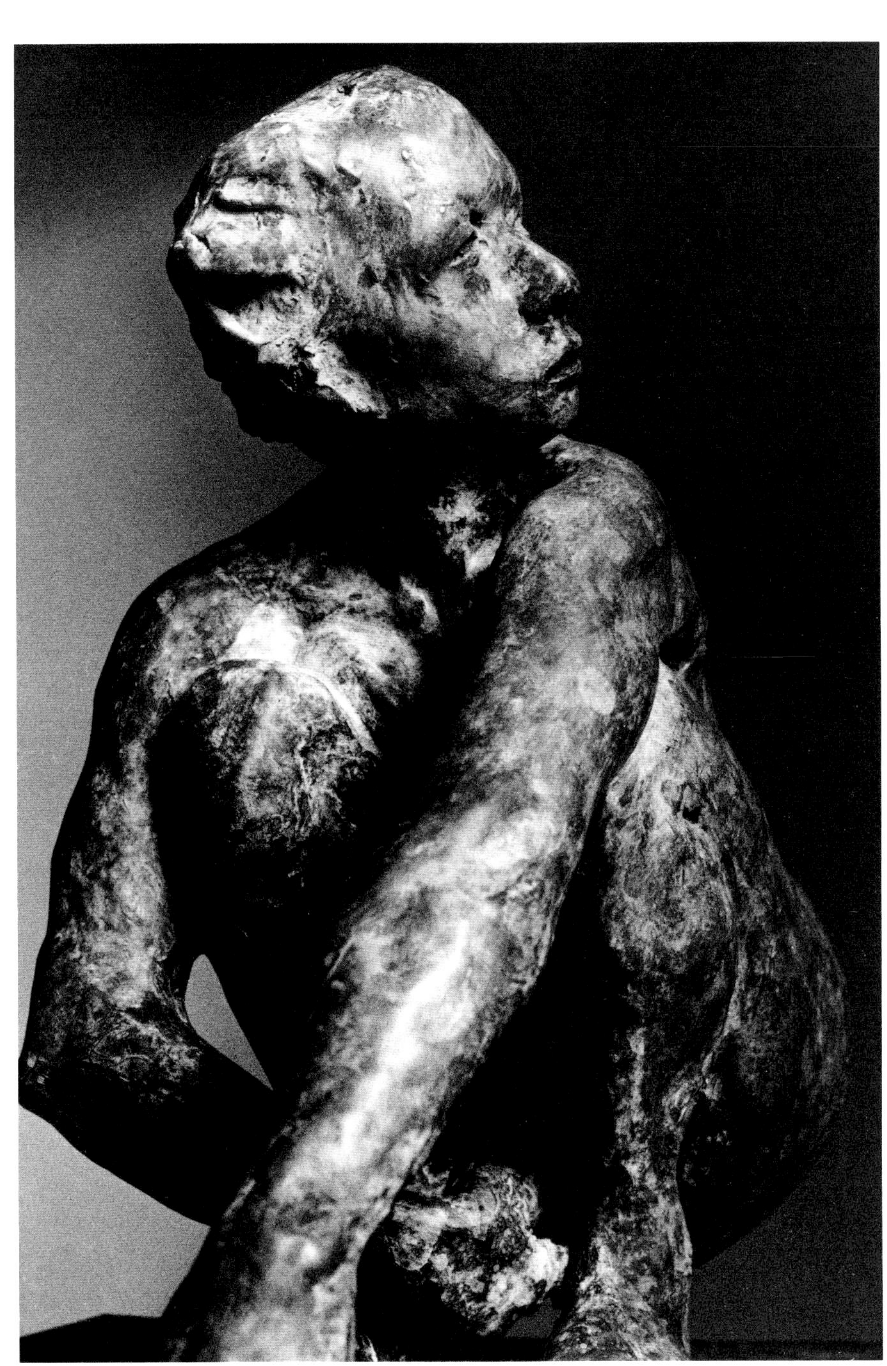

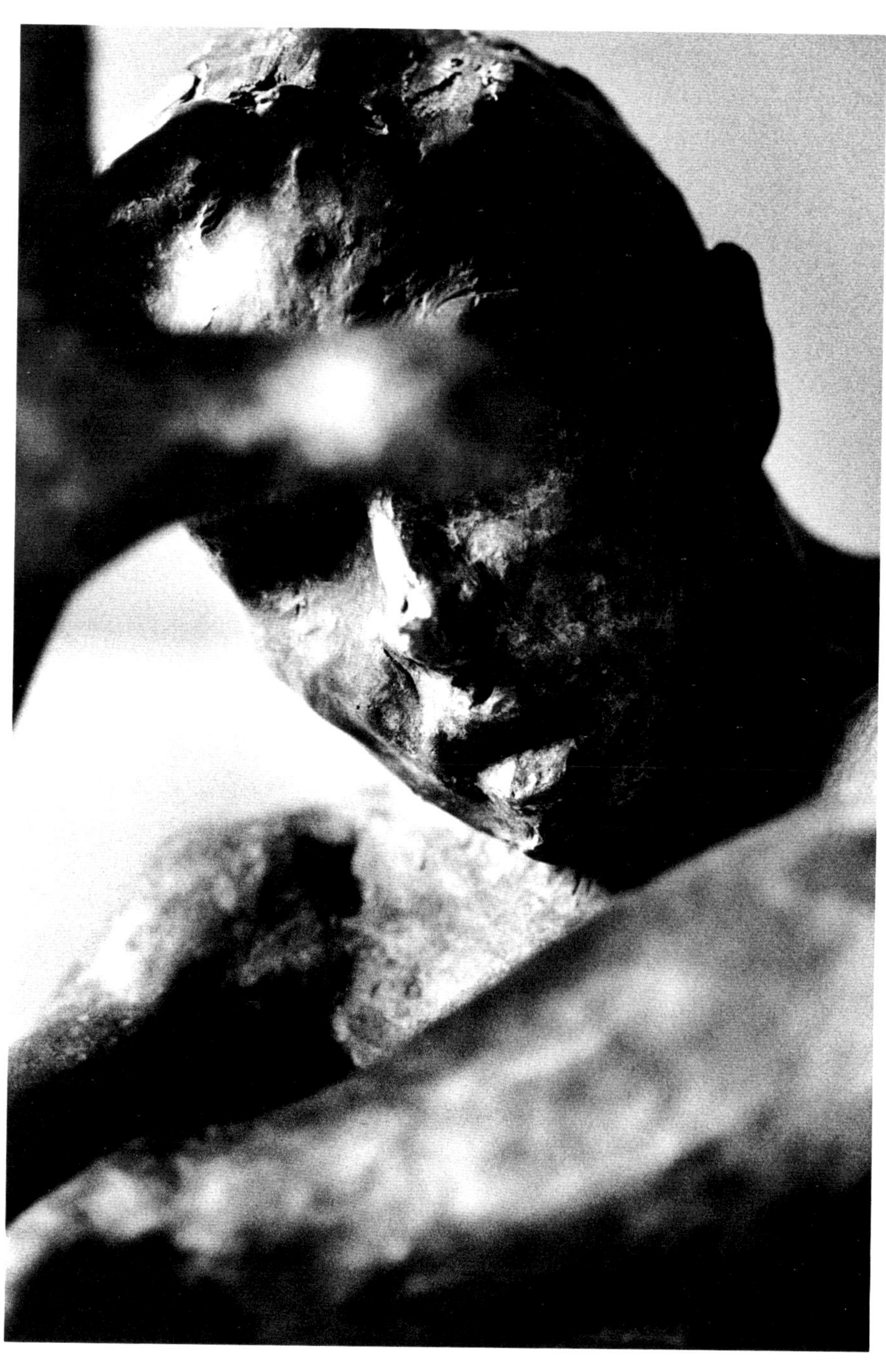

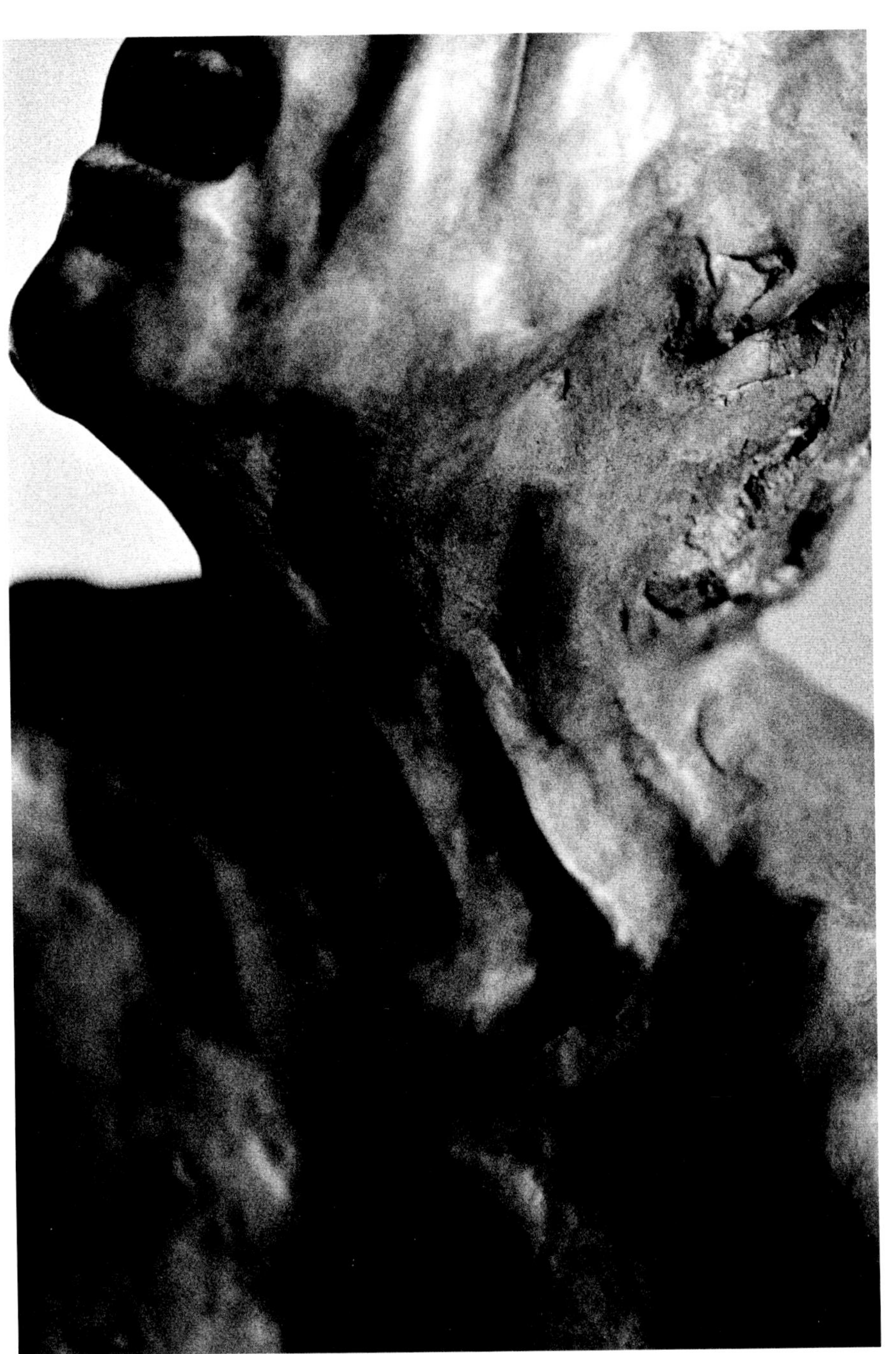

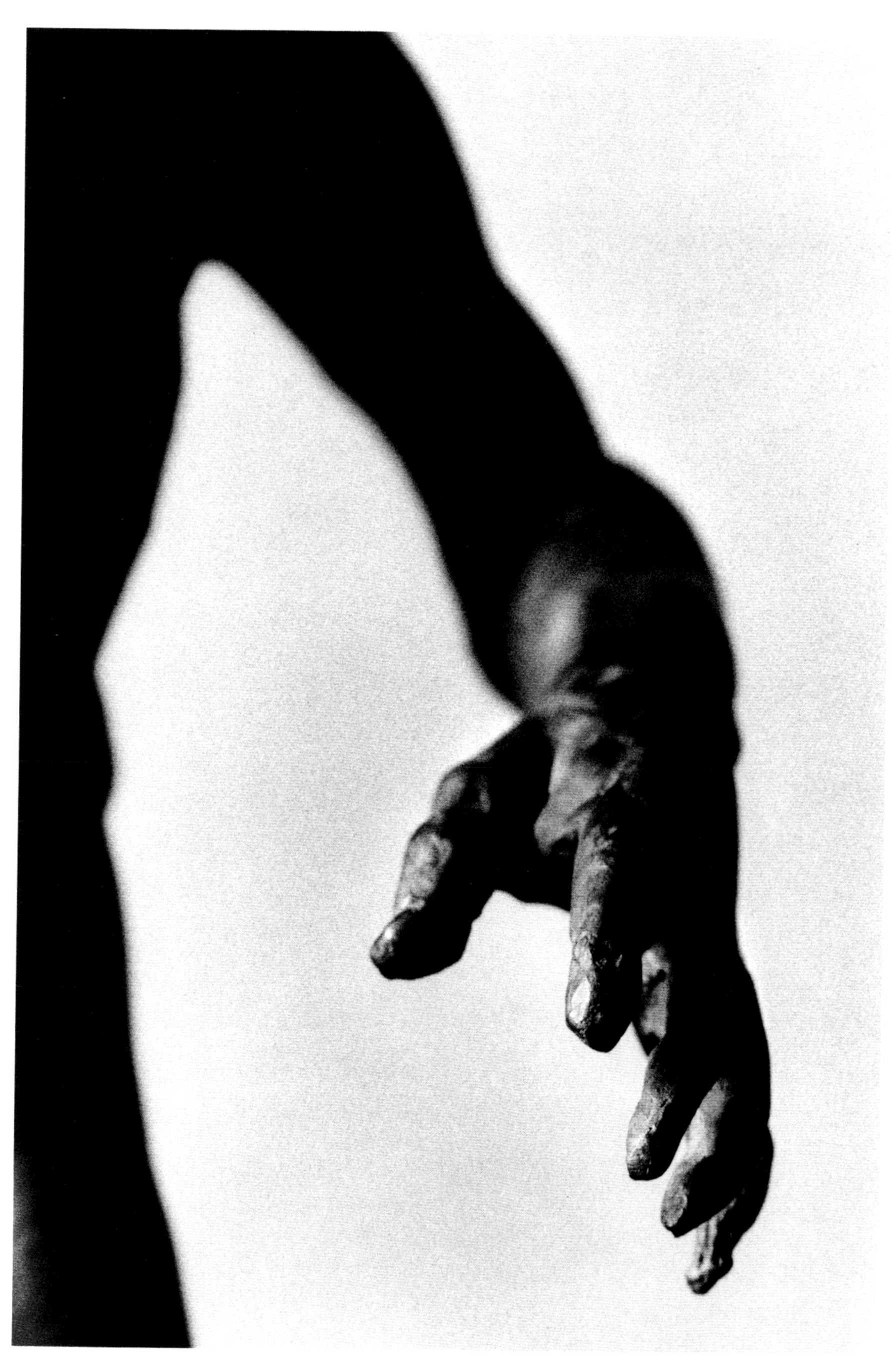

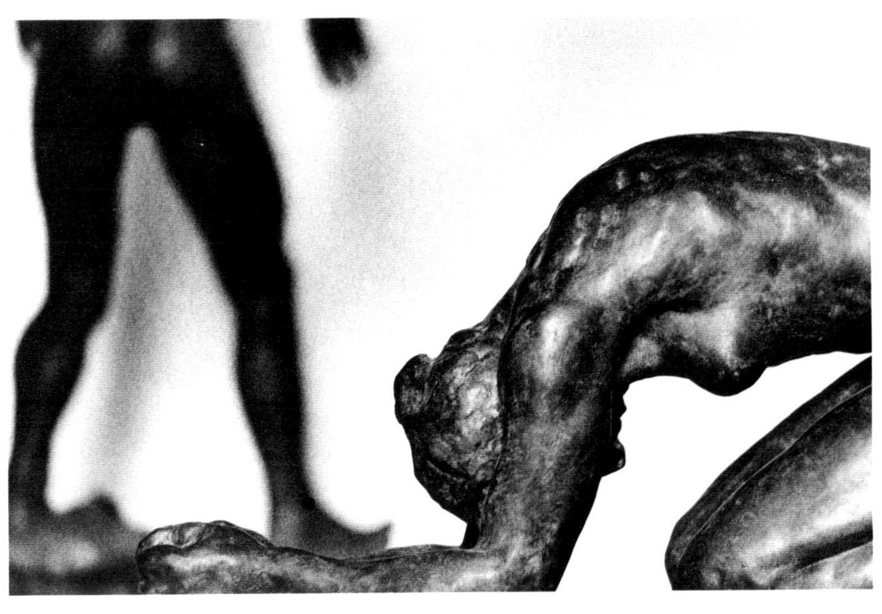

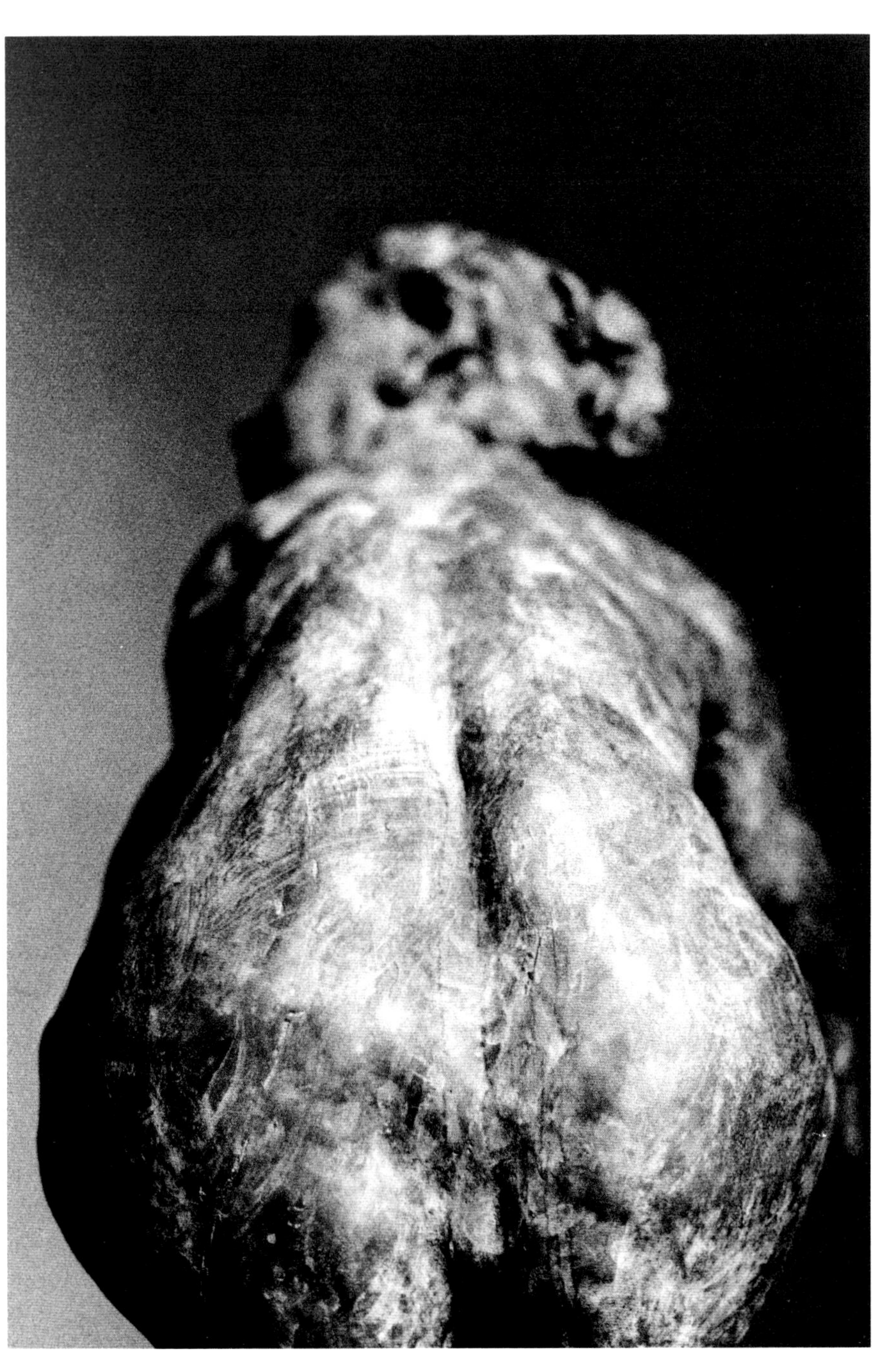

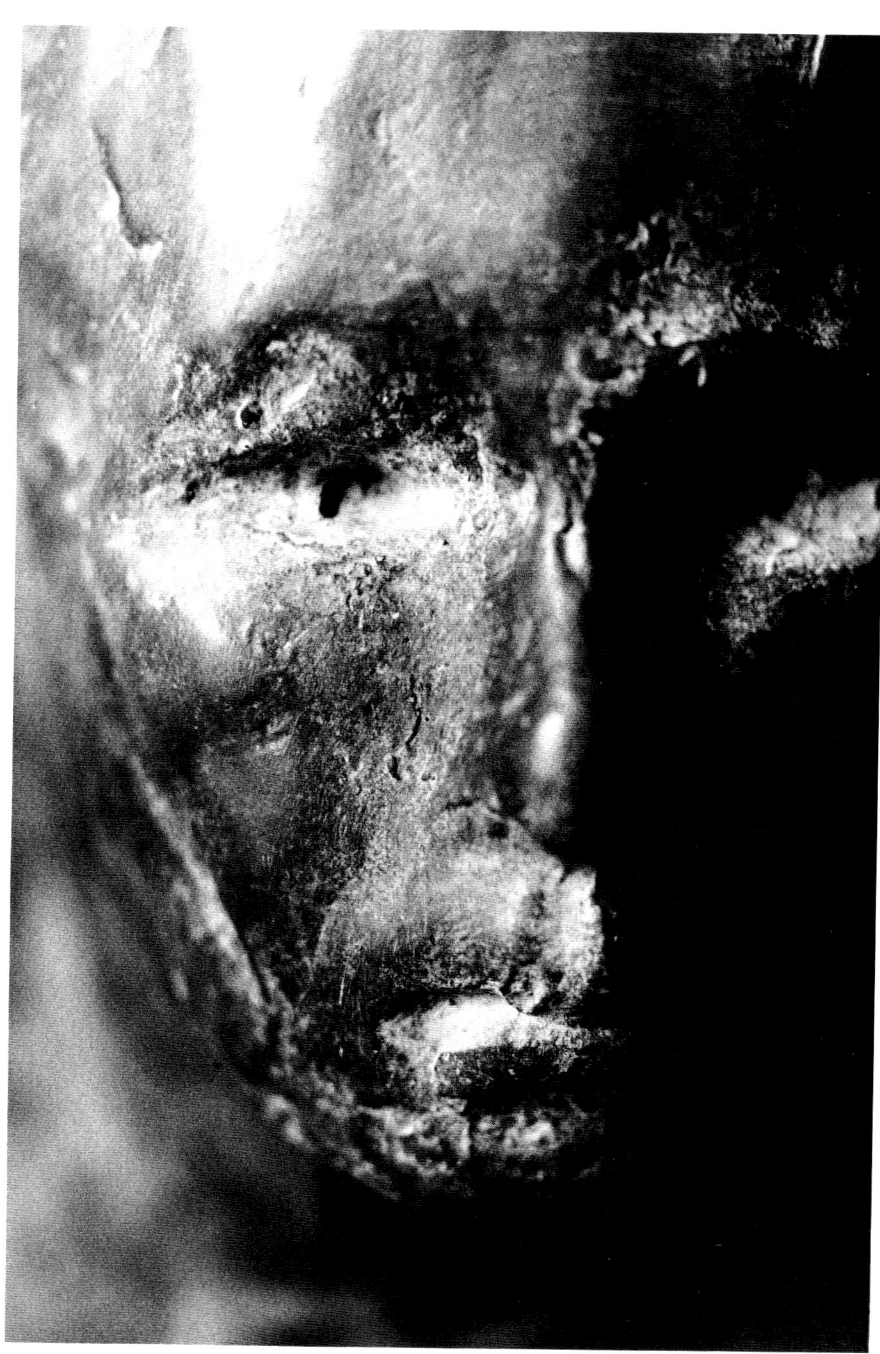

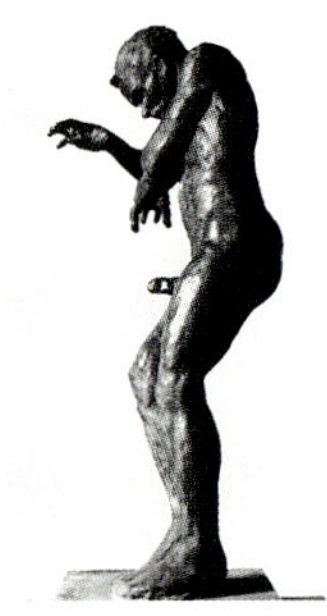

Puppeteer
BRONZE 1997
51 ½ X 18 X 18 ½ INCHES
EDITION 1/3

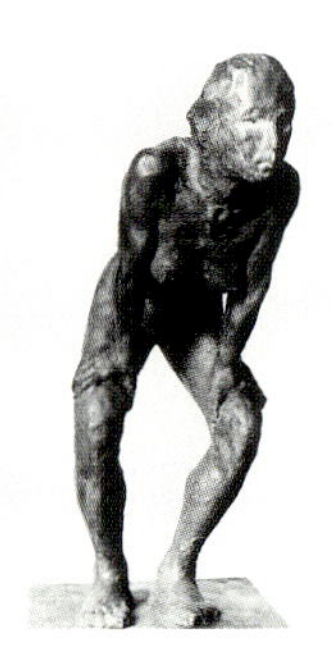

The Watcher
BRONZE 1997
32 X 19 X 14 ½ INCHES
EDITION 1/5

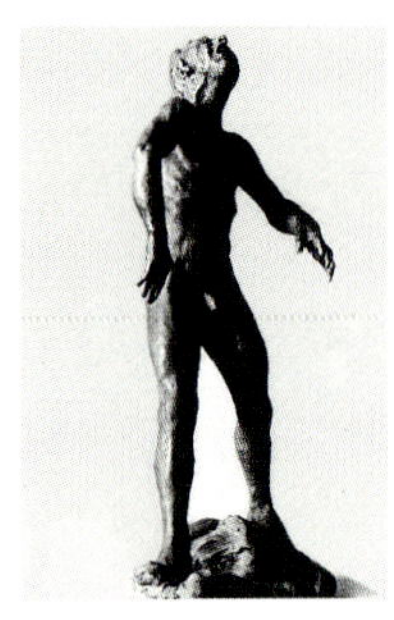

the brave Moment
BRONZE 1997
45 X 22 X 18 INCHES
EDITION 1/5

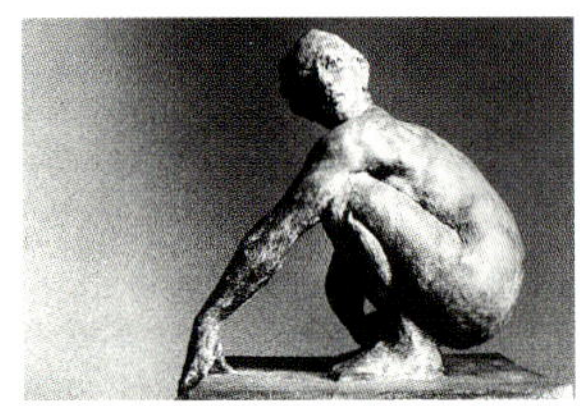

Untitled
BRONZE 1997
21 X 19 X 18 INCHES
EDITION 1/5

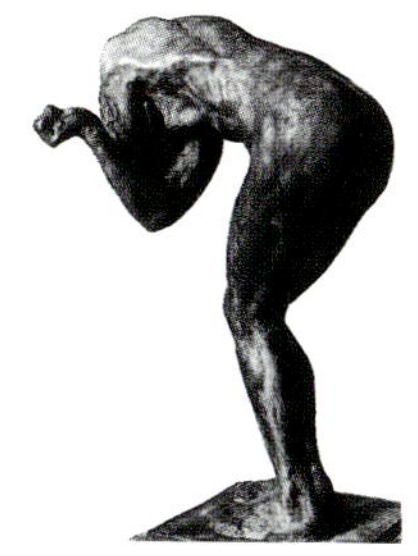

The Weight
BRONZE 1996
31 ½ X 23 X 11 INCHES
EDITION 1/5

The Wait
BRONZE 1997
14 ½ X 20 X 29 ½ INCHES
EDITION 1/5

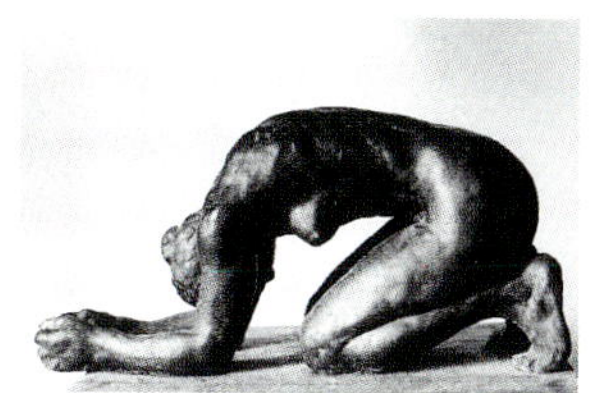

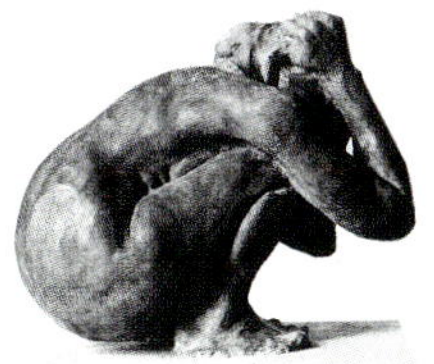

Message of God
BRONZE 1997
21 X 16 ½ X 25 INCHES
EDITION 1/3

Hysterics of Love
BRONZE 1997
21 X 28 X 54 INCHES
EDITION 1/3

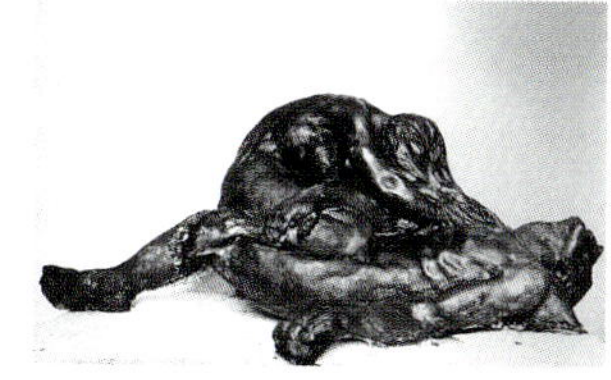

This volume is published on the occasion of the exhibition

ERIC FISCHL: Sculpture

January 15–February 28, 1998

GAGOSIAN GALLERY

980 Madison Avenue, New York, New York 10021

Telephone (212) 744 2313 Fax (212) 772 7962

EDITOR: Ealan Wingate

GAGOSIAN GALLERY COÖRDINATORS:

Amanda Cutter, Lisa Kim, Melissa Lazarov

TYPOGRAPHY AND DESIGN: Kim Spurlock

Printed and bound at The Studley Press, Dalton, Massachusetts

ISBN: 1-880154-18-8

LICC: 97-078226

FRONTIS PHOTOGRAPH: *The Weight* [DETAIL] 1996